ANSWER
WITH TRUTH

THE AMBASSADOR'S FIELD MANUAL FOR
LEADING YOUR FAMILY SPIRITUALLY

DAVID "GOOSE" MILLS

WESTBOW
PRESS®
A DIVISION OF THOMAS NELSON
& ZONDERVAN

WestBow Press books may be ordered through
booksellers or by contacting:

WestBow Press
A Division of Thomas Nelson & Zondervan
1663 Liberty Drive
Bloomington, IN 47403
www.westbowpress.com
844-714-3454

ISBN: 979-8-3850-1618-1 (sc)
ISBN: 979-8-3850-1619-8 (e)

Library of Congress Control Number: 2024900840

Print information available on the last page.

WestBow Press rev. date: 5/24/2024

CONTENTS

Foreword   ix

Acknowledgments   xiii

Introduction   xv

THE PURPOSE OF APOLOGETICS   1

LEADING AT HOME   4

The Three Big Buckets: Relativism,
Pluralism, Scientism   5

WHAT DOES A CHRISTIAN BELIEVE?   13

The Men's Alliance Statement of Faith   14

What Makes Christianity Unique?   15

The Bible   18

MORE THAN A FEELING   23

ANSWERING THE HARD STUFF   26

1. Who Made God?   28

2. Christianity Is Just a Copycat Religion   30

3. You Don't Really Believe Those
   Fairy Tales in the Bible, Do You?   32

4. Christians Just Cherry-Pick the
   Parts of the Bible They Like   34

5. We're Both Atheists When It
    Comes to 99 Percent of All Gods   38
6. Jesus Never Even Claimed to Be God   39
7. Religion Is Responsible for Most
    of the Wars and Atrocities   42
8. The Bible Is Full of Errors and
    Contradictions   45
9. The God of the Old Testament Is
    a Monster!   52
10. Science Has Already Disproved God   55
11. A Lot of Fanatics Will Die for
    Their Faith; That Doesn't Prove
    They're Telling the Truth   60
12. You're Only a Christian Because
    You Were Born in America (or
    Your Parents Are Christian)   61
13. How Could a God Allow All This
    Suffering and Evil in the World?   63
14. Why Do Bad Things Happen to
    Good People?   68
15. Why Does God Send People to
    Hell for Not Believing in Him?   69
16. "Progressive Christianity" and
    Deconstructing Your Faith   70
17. Christians Are Not Supposed to Judge   73

HOW TO SHARE THE GOSPEL   76

FOUR POINTS TO REMEMBER   83

APPENDIX 1: EVIDENCE FOR GOD   85

APPENDIX 2: EVIDENCE FOR CHRISTIANITY   95

APPENDIX 3: THE TWELVE MEN'S ALLIANCE MEMORY
          VERSES   101

APPENDIX 4: HOW TO SHARE THE GOSPEL USING
          ROMANS ROAD   105

APPENDIX 5: WHY ARE YOU A CHRISTIAN?   109

FOREWORD

"Get out of your comfort zone!" These words have been uttered many times by Dave "Goose" Mills in that all-familiar North Carolina accent. Getting out of your comfort zone is the only way to grow and learn.

I met Goose in the fall of 2020. What a crazy time for the world. In the midst of it all, I was introduced to Goose and a very simple ministry designed to bring men out of isolation, out of their comfort zones, and out from behind those façades that some of us had spent our entire lives creating. These weekly gatherings, which included an outdoor thirty-minute workout and a thirty-minute devotion around a fire, were only the beginning of me being pushed outside my own comfort zone. Goose had discovered a brilliant yet simple formula that connected men and formed a bond with one another in a way that I had not experienced since my days in the military.

Since that time, I have seen so many men benefit from belonging to a tribe. Many of them are now some of my closest friends and I will consider brothers.

Swinging sledgehammers, flipping tires, and doing countless burpees before we gathered around a fire to share our real-world struggles as men were only the beginning of my discomfort. There was a quick realization that Goose had more in mind. Sharpening myself physically and spiritually by meeting with my tribe weekly was one thing, but now he was talking about becoming a barbarian ambassador. What was that?

Little did I know that I was about to become the beneficiary of the years of strategic leadership training and experience that Goose acquired over his twenty years in the United States Air Force. This book is an important piece of that leadership, discipleship, and apologetics training.

In Romans, Paul writes, "Do not conform to the pattern of this world but be transformed by the renewing of your mind" (Rom 12:2). This is at the heart of what it means to be a barbarian—someone who refuses to conform to the prevailing culture. Will your neighbors be surprised to find out that you are a follower of Jesus? It's easy to fall into the trap of looking and acting like those around us. But we are called to be different, to be set apart, to be barbarians!

Paul again writes in his second letter to the church in Corinth that we are ambassadors for Christ. "We are therefore Christ's ambassadors, as though God were making his appeal through us. We implore you on Christ's behalf: Be reconciled to God" (2 Cor 5:20). Sometimes, I wonder why he has chosen to reveal himself to the world through people like you and me. I often feel like Moses, unworthy of speaking on behalf of God (Ex 4:10). Maybe you feel the same way. This book will change that.

There are hundreds of books on Christian apologetics that you can choose to read. This one boils it down and presents it in an easy-to-understand format for the common man. This book will provide you with the tools needed to defend and share your faith with more confidence than ever before. Goose has written it to help you on your journey to become the barbarian ambassador that God has designed you to be!

Ray "Thor" Wageman

ACKNOWLEDGMENTS

Almost nothing that you're going to read here is my original idea. I have compiled much of this material from great Christian writers like C. S. Lewis, William Lane Craig, Frank Turek, Greg Koukl, John Lennox, Norman Geisler, Nabeel Qureshi, Lee Strobel, Hugh Ross, Gary Habermas, J. Warner Wallace, Alvin Plantinga, J. P. Moreland, Dan Wallace, James White, Andy Stanley, and Tim Barnett. I sincerely thank these men for the work they've spent their lives doing to share their wisdom and tactics. Reading and listening to them have changed the way I represent Jesus to those around me.

Additionally, I wouldn't have any of this knowledge without Aaron Boykin and Mike Flynn putting together and leading the weekly apologetics group I attend. Aaron's knowledge on Christian apologetics is extraordinary, and I consider it a blessing to learn from him.

Last, writing this book has been my wife Kerry's idea. And for her to think I should write a manual is no small thing since normally she tells me that I need to do less.

INTRODUCTION

You're driving your son and his friend home one evening, and you ask the friend if he goes to church anywhere. He replies, "No, sir, I'm an atheist." Your son looks at you and raises his eyebrows.

The friend continues. "There's just no way anyone can know if there's actually an afterlife or not, and I don't believe all the stories in the Bible anyway."

You're at lunch with your buddy and his father, and the television in the restaurant shows a commercial for the Bible on DVD. Your friend's dad says, "There are so many errors and contradictions in the Bible, I don't know how anybody can actually believe it."

You're sharing a rental car with a coworker when they ask, "You're a Christian, right?" You say yes, wondering where this is about to go.

They reply, "I just can't be a Christian because a loving God would want to stop all the evil in the world, and a powerful God could stop the evil. So, if there's any god at all, he's clearly not all loving and all powerful."

Will these moments catch you off guard? Will you be flustered with a half-baked reply? Will you even speak up at all?

The problem is 70 percent of Christian teenagers claim they are no longer Christians after their first year of college.[1] This shows that fathers are probably spending more time playing fun games and eating pizza with their kids than teaching them what they believe and why. My goal is to help you teach your kids that Christianity doesn't require you to check your intellect at the door. Jesus commands us to love God with all our mind. So, we're not being fully loving if we don't engage our intellect in our faith.

If we are to become spiritual leaders in our home, then we must be so confident and so prepared that we look forward to the tough questions. Far from catching us off guard and flustered, these moments are a gift from God!

I know what you're thinking. You think that you aren't qualified to lead anyone spiritually. You know all your sins and failures, and you feel you aren't good enough to lead your family. You're afraid they'll see right through you and call you a hypocrite.

Here are three tips to help you lead your family spiritually:

Tip 1: You're not perfect. Lead anyway. Paul wrote in the book of Romans that every person has sinned and fallen short of the glory of God. Satan wants to remind you of your sins, throw them back in your face, and get you to stay quiet on the sidelines.

Tip 2: Admit your faults. Tell your family that you know you're not perfect by a long stretch but that you want to help them fully understand why Jesus died on a cross and how that changes literally everything.

Tip 3: Read the answer key. If you already know the questions they're going to ask you, and you are prepared with the answers beforehand, then you'll be much more confident and willing to lead others spiritually. This manual is designed to give you those answers and the confidence that goes with them.

News flash! We are ambassadors! According to 2 Corinthians 5:20, we are commanded to be ambassadors for Jesus. And our family is our first place of assignment.

If you were the American ambassador to China, you would certainly prepare by learning the answers to the questions you would likely be asked, right? You'd brush up on the GNP, trade laws, and regional military forces, and you'd be prepared to answer questions like What makes America different from other nations?

I'm quite sure that God had that preparation in mind when he chose to call us ambassadors. What kind of ambassador for Jesus will we be if we don't know what makes us different from a Mormon or a Muslim? What kind of ambassador will we be if we are caught off guard by the most common questions that people have been asking for years? Ambassadors for Jesus Christ should know both the questions and the answers to accurately represent their King.

MY PERSONAL STORY

I spent far too many years not speaking out for Jesus because I was afraid of appearing stupid or hypocritical if I opened my mouth. When we don't know what questions will be asked, and we don't have any answers prepared, we make terrible ambassadors. It was not until I joined an apologetics group several years ago that my mind began growing in knowledge of how to answer the tough questions that I'd been avoiding my whole life. I learned that all questions (and accusations) fit into only a few different categories (or buckets) and that each bucket was filled with illogical arguments propped up by rhetoric.

My confidence in my own faith began to grow as I learned that Christianity actually does have the answers. The answers are all there! They are logical, consistent, and coherent. It's just that most Christians are such bad ambassadors that the world doesn't know this. Imagine if all the US ambassadors to China for the last fifty years had been high school dropouts. We wouldn't be surprised if China didn't think very highly of America.

The reason many Americans today are turning away from Christianity has nothing to do with the message of Jesus. It has everything to do with his ambassadors!

The word *apologetics* comes from the Greek work *apologia*—meaning a well-reasoned argument. Some Christians think apologetics is a separate discipline that is only appealing to certain people. That view is flat wrong. If you are a Christian, then you'd better be an apologist. The apostle Peter calls us all out in 1 Peter 3:15: "Always be prepared to give an answer to everyone who asks you to give the reason for the hope that you have. But do this with gentleness and respect." We simply cannot be bold ambassadors for Jesus without being "prepared to give an answer."

My goal in writing this is to help prepare you to give an answer and become a better ambassador for Jesus of Nazareth. May this be a resource that helps you boldly and accurately lead your family spiritually.

David "Goose" Mills

THE PURPOSE OF APOLOGETICS

As Alister McGrath says in *Mere Apologetics*, the goal of apologetics is not to win arguments or argue someone into Christianity. Apologetics is about removing the obstacles that are in people's way. Sometimes, those obstacles have to do with science, suffering, miracles, or history. Once their path is cleared of obstacles, it is then that evangelism invites the person to walk down the cleared path.[2] Apologetics and evangelism work hand in hand.

In Acts 2, Peter used an apologetic argument as he spoke to fellow Jews. He tailored his language according to his audience by citing Old Testament (OT) predictions of a Messiah and referring to Abraham, Isaac,

ANSWER WITH TRUTH

and Jacob. These words and themes would not be persuasive to anyone other than a Jewish audience. So, Peter was not using a one-size-fits-all message about Jesus, but rather he used an argument that would be effective with that specific audience.

Likewise, as Paul spoke in Acts 17 to a Greek audience, he did not use any of those Old Testament terms because they would place more obstacles rather than remove them. Instead, Paul quoted a Greek poet and identified Jesus Christ as the "unknown God" to whom the Greeks had an altar. This was truly speaking the language of his audience![3]

Just as Peter and Paul tailored their words so that they would be clearly received by their audience, so, too, should we learn to speak the language of our audience. We must meet people where they are, use words they understand and arguments they will find persuasive, and remove the obstacles that they personally struggle with. This requires us to do a lot of listening before we speak. For example, if a person believes the Bible is a fourth-century invention written to control the masses, then it will be futile to say to them that the Bible says such and such. You must first remove the obstacle between them and the reliability of New Testament (NT) manuscripts.

We will fail as ambassadors if we do not first get to know our audience, ask them what they believe, ask them if they've considered Christianity, and if they've rejected it, ask them why. And just as Paul used arguments familiar to the Greeks in Athens, so we must use arguments that resonate today.

LEADING AT HOME

The most important battle that we'll ever fight is for the souls of our children. Yet, somehow, we spend more time taking them to soccer practice and talking about their grades in school than discussing with them what we believe and why. I think this neglect comes from not knowing what to say exactly and a fear of their responding with a question (or accusation) that makes us look foolish.

News flash! There are only three main categories. Most objections to Christianity that your kids will have can fit into one of three buckets. The way questions are worded may change over the years, but the three major buckets don't. If you learn how to address each bucket and to recognize in which bucket your kid's objections go, then (like 1 Peter 3:15 commands) you'll always be prepared to give an answer.

For each objection to Christianity, I will give you both a short answer, which is what you'll want to use at the dinner table or around the watercooler, and then a deeper answer for if that person is genuinely seeking truth and wants to follow up with you later.

THE THREE BIG BUCKETS

BUCKET 1: RELATIVISM

Relativism says there is no truth. You can't really know anything for certain. You have your truth, and I have mine. Whatever works for you is fine, and whatever works for someone else is acceptable too. It's all good. Don't try to push your truth on others. Everything is relative.

The relativism bucket is fast growing in America. It's a crowd-pleaser, and using it makes you sound like the cool, laid-back peacemaker. It works great at parties, and for that reason, your kids might be attracted to it at some point.

Short answer: Is it true that there is no truth? Do you know for certain that you can't know anything for certain? Is relativism true for all people everywhere? You see, the problem with relativism is that it is logically self-defeating. As soon as you apply the claim of relativism to itself, it cuts off the very limb that it's sitting on.

You might also ask them if it's true that George Washington was the first president of the United States. So, there are *historical truths*. Is the Nile River in Egypt? So, there are *geographic truths*. Does two plus two equal four? So, there are *mathematical truths*. Do two hydrogen molecules and one oxygen molecule make water? So, there are *scientific truths*. So, I guess not *everything* is relative, right? And, since we've all just agreed that there are historic, geographic, mathematic, and scientific truths, isn't it possible that there are also moral and religious truths?

Deeper answer: Is racism, discrimination, and child sex trafficking objectively wrong for all people everywhere?

If they say yes, then they are admitting that relativism is not true by confessing that universal objective morality does exist (more on that as evidence for the existence of God in appendix 1). If they say no, then they are indeed being consistent, but they are admitting that all heinous injustices (such as genocide and torture) are merely matters of personal opinion. And if those are just matters of opinion (like your favorite ice cream), then they shouldn't try to stop others from doing them. Ouch!

Bottom line: If your worldview cannot condemn genocide, torture, and racism (and it's logically self-defeating), then you seriously need to get yourself a new worldview.

If your daughter says she's become a relativist, it is highly likely that she's never really considered it this far. She's probably just repeating a bumper sticker philosophy picked up during her freshman year of college, and she's never been challenged on it. (This makes *them* bad ambassadors for relativism.) So, tread lightly. Don't try to rub their face in it. Just lovingly explain the logical problem as well as the deeper implications of the relativistic worldview.

BUCKET 2: PLURALISM

Pluralism says that all paths lead to the same place. We all worship the same God; we just know him by different names. It's arrogant to think that only your path is the correct one. Religions are like blind men feeling an elephant. One thinks it's like a rope, the other a tree trunk, another a wall, but they're all describing different parts of the same thing.

Pluralism is the ultimate crowd-pleaser. It's so warm and fuzzy, progressive, and universal. Golly gee, I sure do hope we're all still pals. Pluralism makes me think of Matthew 7:13, "Enter through the narrow gate; for the gate is wide and the way is broad that leads to destruction, and there are many who enter through it. For the gate is small and the way is narrow that leads to life, and there are few who find it."

Short answer: What did Jesus have to say about other paths? (If you're holding a mic, then you can drop it at this point.) John 14:6 tells us that Jesus said, "I am the way, the truth, and the life, and no one comes to the Father except through me." So, as C. S. Lewis famously said, either Jesus is the only way or he's a liar.[4] But he clearly isn't one of many good ways.

Deeper answer: Pluralism violates the law of logic known as the law of noncontradiction, which states that something cannot be both true and false at the same time. For example, the light in the room can be on, or the light can be off, but, logically, it cannot be both. While it is logically possible that all religions are false or that only one religion is true, they cannot all be true since one of them (Christianity) makes a claim to be the *only* way.

Christianity is exclusive. It excludes all other gods, paths, good works, idols, and lucky charms. First Timothy 2:5 says, "For there is one God and one mediator between God and mankind, the man Christ Jesus." And Acts 4:12 says, "Salvation is found in no one else, for there is no other name under heaven given to mankind by which we must be saved."

Bottom line: If your worldview contradicts logic and calls Jesus a liar, then you seriously need to get yourself a new worldview.

So, if your son comes home from college saying things in this pluralism bucket, just lovingly remind him that Jesus made an exclusive truth claim, so he's either the only way or he's a liar.

BUCKET 3: SCIENTISM

Also called materialism or naturalism, scientism states that only science gives us truth. Everything else—such as religion, philosophy, and morals—is just opinions. Molecules and atoms are all that exist in this universe, and if it isn't made of those, then it's just your opinion.

If relativism is the stoner at the party that questions whether consciousness really exists, and pluralism is the guy who just wants everyone to get along, then scientism is wearing a tweed jacket and smoking a pipe. Scientism is condescending to all other academic disciplines by claiming to have exclusive access to knowledge and truth. (And they think Christians are arrogant!)

Short answer: The claim of scientism is also logically self-defeating. Can you prove through a scientific experiment that only science gives us truth? Or is that very statement just a personal opinion about science? Ouch. Scientism itself is not even science but rather a philosophical theory about science.[5] The person making the statement has no testable, scientific evidence that scientism is true. They can't prove that the supernatural does not exist. That's outside the realm of science.

Deeper answer: Do you believe that justice, love, logic, and mathematics exist? Are they made of molecules and atoms? What about your love for your wife, mom, and so forth? Is that real? Can its atoms be weighed or measured?

In fact, there are many moral truths that we know with *greater* certainty than scientific truths. For example, our definition of *planet* keeps changing, our knowledge of electrons has changed many times in the last seventy years, and as we learn new things, it changes what we thought we knew.[6] There's an entire Wikipedia page on superseded theories. But there is nothing that we will learn in the future to change our moral laws that rape, genocide, kidnapping, and so forth are wrong. Those truths cannot be tested through science, yet we know them with greater certainty. Why is that? Where have these moral laws come from? (At this point, if they begin to claim it is a social construct, refer back to relativism.)

Some materialists will claim that all your thoughts, feelings, and emotions are merely the products of chemical reactions in your brain. Then ask them if a person who sexually molests a child is responsible for their crime. Or are they just "dancing to their DNA" as Richard Dawkins suggests? If your son or daughter claims that all thoughts are merely the product of chemical reactions in their brain, then ask them why they trust their thoughts to come to that very conclusion.[7]

Bottom line: If your worldview claims to be 100 percent scientific, yet it cannot be scientifically proved itself, then you need to find yourself a new worldview. And if it claims that pedophiles are just dancing to their DNA, then you need to run from it!

WHAT DOES A CHRISTIAN BELIEVE?

Now that we've shot holes in the three buckets of relativism, pluralism, and scientism, let's talk about the correct worldview. Let's define what exactly Christianity is. While it's easy to get lost in the weeds of the age of the earth, the methods of baptism, or the five points of Calvinism, those things have nothing to do with becoming a Christian. Christians debate all kinds of minor details. So, let's make sure we're clear on the major point. Here's our statement of faith that really hits what's important.

THE MEN'S ALLIANCE STATEMENT OF FAITH

The Holy Bible, and only the Bible, is the authoritative Word of God. There is one God, eternally existent in three persons: Father, Son, and Holy Spirit. These three are coequal and coeternal.

Jesus Christ is God the Son, the second person of the Trinity. On the earth, Jesus was 100 percent God and 100 percent man. He is the only man ever to have lived a sinless life. He was born of a virgin, performed miracles, died on the cross for mankind, and thus atoned for our sins through the shedding of his blood. He rose from the dead on the third day according to the scriptures, ascended to the right hand of the Father, and will return again in power and glory.

We are saved by grace through faith in Jesus Christ: his death, burial, and resurrection. Salvation is a gift from God, not a result of our good works or of any human efforts.

WHAT MAKES CHRISTIANITY UNIQUE?

A lot of high school and college students are under the impression that all religions are basically the same. This is because they are completely ignorant about what different religions teach. While it's true that there are a few very superficial similarities between religions (like they all have a version of the Golden Rule), their differences are far more important than their similarities. A glass of water may be 99 percent similar to a glass of water with one drop of cyanide in it, but believe me, that 1 percent difference is a life-and-death issue.

So here are some key points to illustrate the absolute uniqueness of Christianity.

1. Christianity is the only non-works-based religion in the world. Mormons, Jews, Buddhists, Hindus, and Muslims are all trying to keep laws, commands, rules, teachings, and pillars to earn their way to paradise, heaven, or nirvana.

2. Christianity alone teaches that you can never ever be good enough to get yourself to heaven.

That's why our Savior had to come down to earth and rescue us. Ephesians 2:8–9 says, "For it is by grace you have been saved through faith—and this is not from yourselves, it is the gift of God—not by works, so that no one can boast." Believe. That's it (see Acts 16:31).

3. Christianity is based on a single historical event that occurred in the spring of AD 33—the resurrection of Jesus after being crucified by the Romans. This event was verified by over five hundred witnesses over a forty-day period (1 Cor 15). These witnesses wrote about it, translated it, circulated it all around the world, made no money, died painfully, never recanted, and started the largest movement in all human history over their claim to having seen a man rise from the dead. Notice how the *teachings* of Jesus did not change their lives. They denied him and ran away after hearing his teachings. But it was the *resurrection* that changed their lives. No other religion claims anything similar.

4. It's the only religion that has a coherent, consistent answer to all of life's biggest questions.

Why are we here? Where have we come from? Where are we going? Why is there suffering and pain? Why do bad things happen to good people? Who is Jesus? Why is his tomb empty? Some worldviews answer a couple of these questions. Others answer only one. Some religions deny the question even exists. (For example, Hinduism teaches there is no suffering and evil; it's all an illusion.[8] Tell that to a woman who's just been raped. If your worldview says there is no evil, then you seriously need a new worldview.)

5. It is the only religion not based on a book or anyone's teachings. Without the Book of Mormon, you have no Mormons. Without the Koran, you have no Muslims. Without the Torah, you have no one practicing Judaism. Without the Vedas, there will be no Hindus. And without the teachings of Buddha, there will not be Buddhists. But if there had never been a Bible, there would still be Christians. Because ...

THE BIBLE

Here's a question you may have never asked yourself: Do you have to *believe the Bible* to be a Christian? Think about this: were there Christians before there was a Bible? Obviously. Early Christians had no Bible. Can a person be a Christian if they're illiterate? What if they have no Bible in their language or have only a New Testament?

We need to be crystal clear on the only requirement for becoming a Christian, and that is *believing in the atoning death and resurrection of Jesus.* So, we can conclude that reading the Bible is not a prerequisite for becoming a Christian. What about the Old Testament, the Torah as the Jews call it? Does your daughter have to believe that every story in it is literal? Is believing that Lot's wife turned into an actual pillar of salt a requirement for becoming a Christian? What if your son thinks the six-day creation story in Genesis is meant to be poetic and figurative, not literal? Does that mean they're not Christians? Of course not! Did Paul tell the Roman guard in Acts chapter 16 that he had to believe the stories of Noah and the ark and Jonah and the fish? No. He simply told him, "Believe on the Lord Jesus Christ and you will be saved."

Remember this: Christianity is *not* like a Jenga tower where if you can pull out one piece, it will all collapse.[9] Christianity has its foundation in just one thing—the resurrection of Jesus. So, if anyone wants to disprove Christianity, they must disprove the resurrection. And people have been trying to do that for nearly two thousand years without success.

I ask these questions about the Bible because most American Christians haven't thought them through. But it is paramount to know, if we're going to be good ambassadors, exactly what it is that makes a person a Christian. Christianity is based on one belief: *that Jesus died and rose again to pay for your sins.* Period.

Romans 10:9 says, "If you declare with your mouth, 'Jesus is LORD,' and believe in your heart that God raised him from the dead, you will be saved."

John 3:16 reiterates that "whoever believes in Him will be saved."

Believe that Jesus Christ has died and risen again to pay for *your* sins. That's it. There is no laundry list.

The reason I'm telling you this about the Bible is so that you'll be a better ambassador to your kid when they come home from school saying they aren't a Christian anymore because they no longer believe in the parting of the Red Sea or in Adam and Eve. I want to equip you for that conversation with tactic 1.

TACTIC 1—DON'T TAKE THE OT BAIT

Don't get bogged down in the Torah. If your son or daughter says they aren't a Christian because of Noah and the ark or Jonah and the fish and so forth, just simply inform them that *those stories are not essential for Christianity. You're a Christian because of the resurrection of Jesus Christ*, not because you believe that Joshua commanded the sun to stand still.

This is a tactical maneuver to sidestep a roadblock and continue on course. If you spent an hour explaining archaeological evidence for a global flood and detailing how, based on the dimensions of the ark (300 × 50 × 30 cubits), all the animals could fit in the ark (which could hold 450 shipping containers) with room to spare, they will just bring up a different issue. Don't get caught in the weeds of trying to prove all the miracles of the Old Testament. Sidestep them. They are not the real reason for someone not being a Christian.

A good question to ask a family member who brings up Noah or Jonah is this: if hypothetically it could be proved that this event happened, would you worship Jesus? I believe you will find that everyone says no. They will just bring up something else they have a problem with.

A good approach is to say, "I doubt that you're turning away from Jesus because of stories found in the Torah. Why don't you tell me what's really keeping you from Christianity?"

News flash! Romans chapter 1 tells us that what can be known about God is clear to everyone. All people see creation and know in their hearts that there is a God. But some people choose to suppress that truth so that they can continue sinning and pretend they are not accountable to a creator.

Let's face it, most college students don't want to follow Jesus because they want to have sex outside of marriage with whomever they want. But since they're not going to admit that, they need to make up something that sounds better, something from one of the buckets. That's what is really keeping people from Christianity—not Balam's talking donkey (Nm 22).

When I am sharing my faith with friends or family, I will allow them the possibility that whatever Old Testament story they bring up may be metaphorical or figurative. I'll concede that the six-day creation account might be using poetic language, not literal.[10] (Read *Seven Days That Divide the World* by Lennox if you want to go deeper on this topic.) I'll allow that I don't know if some of the stories are meant to be literal or not. Maybe. I don't know. They're not really vital to Christianity. I'm not an expert on the Torah; I'm not Jewish. I'm a Christian because of the resurrection of Jesus.

Keep bringing it back to the main point. (Later, I will give you another tactic for handling OT story questions more directly.)

MORE THAN A FEELING

There's nothing wrong with feeling in your heart that Christianity is true or sensing that there is a God. I firmly believe that the Holy Spirit guides us and nudges us and that sometimes we are given divine inspiration that leads us to truth. However, I don't think that these feelings help anyone who didn't feel them personally. They're intended only for the recipient. Therefore, they don't make for a compelling case for Christ (to borrow a term from Mr. Strobel). Additionally, if we open up the floodgates of following our feelings, then we're not going to like where that leads. Muslims and Mormons have feelings too. Does that mean *their* religion is true?

So, when it comes to being able to "give an answer to everyone who asks you to give the reason for the hope

23

that you have" (1 Pt 3:15), we need to have something more than just a story about a feeling we had at camp one summer or when we've had a near-death experience and so on. After all, Mormons are notorious for claiming they have the truth because of a "burning in their bosom." And Muslims can have a feeling that they are right. And so can Hindus and atheists. So, let's not just join in the feelings party. Let's have good reasons for our faith. Let's have evidence.

Now, if you are a brand-new Christian who has just recently made the decision to become a follower of Jesus Christ, feelings may be all you have. And there's nothing wrong with that. But as we move beyond newborn babes in Christ to becoming ambassadors, we need to have more to offer.

Imagine again that you're the US ambassador to Russia, and you're asked why you love America so much. I hope that you'll have more to offer than just saying that you feel deep in your heart that it's the greatest country ever. I hope that you'll be able to explain its unparalleled Constitution, its Bill of Rights with First and Second Amendments that no other country enjoys. I hope you'll explain our free-market capitalism and our "marketplace of ideas" as Oliver Wendell Holmes has described.

So it is with Christianity also. When given the opportunity to answer why it is that you're a Christian, I hope you knock it out of the park by explaining why it's unique (p. 15) and what the evidence is (appendixes 1 and 2).

Ultimately, we're not Christians because of blind faith or warm feelings. We're Christians because it's the best explanation of the evidence. See appendix 5 for a complete and compelling answer to "Why are you a Christian?"

ANSWERING THE HARD STUFF

As previously stated, to be a good ambassador, we must know what questions people typically ask and prepare ourselves with the answers beforehand. We cannot be good ambassadors for Jesus if we haven't even read our opponent's playbook. After you read the books written by prominent atheists, watch videos of them debating Christians. Watch the popular internet videos where trendy young atheists try to debunk Christianity. You'll start to realize that they really don't have any arguments. It's a lot of rhetoric, ad hominem attacks, and straw man fallacies. And, honestly, that's encouraging. It's great to realize that the enemy is weaponless. How can it really be any other way? We have *the* Truth on our side.

But we must still be prepared to help our family see this. And no matter how unwilling a skeptical son or daughter may be to listen to your points, it is still worth your time because you're planting a seed. And, sometimes, it's the bystander (the younger sibling) listening who might be influenced the most.

News flash! Every person falls somewhere on this continuum:

Truth → God → Miracles → Resurrection of Jesus[11]

As you listen to a person, ask them questions to figure out where they are on the continuum. Meet them where they are. For example, the relativist is stuck at the beginning, thinking that truth does not exist. The atheist is stuck on the next step, thinking that God does not exist. And the materialist/naturalist believes that miracles are not possible. Jews, Muslims, Mormons, and many others all believe in truth, God, and miracles; however, they do not recognize the resurrection of Jesus as their saving payment for their sin. When you realize where someone is on this continuum, you can more successfully talk to them without having your words fall on deaf ears. (I'll give you an example in some of the tough questions below.)

Also, keep in mind that this continuum is circular because Jesus is the truth. And if the resurrection has occurred, then there is obviously a God, and miracles are possible.

So, here are some of the most common questions or accusations that an ambassador can expect to face along with some ways you can answer to help you get the person thinking.

1. WHO MADE GOD?

If you're thinking that this sounds too silly to be real, think again. Richard Dawkins asked this question while debating John Lennox, and many intelligent people actually think this is a real stumper. So, take them seriously and treat them gently and with love if they ask you this.

TACTIC 2—ASK, "WHAT DO YOU MEAN BY _____?"

If you are asked, "Who made God?" you first need to back up and define your terms. They may be thinking of God as a man with a long white beard who sits on a cloud. For that reason, if you're asked, "Do you believe in God?" or "Who made God?" ask them, "What do you mean by God?"[12] We want to make sure we're talking about the same thing.

It may need explaining that "God" is the name we give to the eternal, immaterial, powerful being who has caused the universe to come into existence out of nothing (Aristotle's "uncaused first cause").

Whatever created space, time, and matter had to be spaceless, timeless, and immaterial. It had to be conscious to decide to create. It had to be personal to create relationships. It had to be loving to give us a need and capacity for love. So, whatever this all-powerful, eternal, loving, personal, conscious thing is that has created the universe and everything in it is what we call *God*. He has no beginning, for he is outside time (in the same way an author is outside the book they are writing). Something must be eternal because if there was ever a time when nothing existed, then nothing would exist today. (More on this in statement 10).

Side note: If anyone questions why we use the pronouns *he* and *him* for God, it is simply because that is God's preferred pronoun. God has chosen it for himself in his book, not us. And we should respect a person's preferred pronoun, right?

So, no one made God. God is eternal. He has no beginning and no end. That is very difficult for us humans to comprehend. But if God could be fully understood by mere mortals like us, then he wouldn't be much of a God.

2. CHRISTIANITY IS JUST A COPYCAT RELIGION

There have been legends of dying and rising saviors throughout various periods such as Osiris, Horus, and Mithras. The story of Jesus is just another one of these recycled stories. It's nothing new.

TACTIC 3—ASK, "HOW DID YOU COME TO THAT CONCLUSION?"[13]

Ask them, "How did you come to that conclusion?" or "What manuscripts or texts have you read about Osiris and Mithras?" (Hint: They haven't read any. They're repeating something they heard on YouTube.) Make them support their claim. And most of what's out there is completely false. For example, you may hear things like Osiris was born of a virgin, had twelve disciples, was crucified, and rose on the third day and so forth. This is false. Just ask them where they have gotten their information on Osiris. There are no ancient manuscripts that confirm these similarities. (For example, the "twelve disciples" similarity is based entirely on a piece of artwork that depicts Mithras with the twelve zodiac signs around him.) Just ask, "Where are you getting this from?" The Mithraic religion has no *early* texts. And its only texts at all are dated *after* Jesus of Nazareth, so if there's any copying, it's copying similarities *from* Christianity.

I will also remind the skeptic that, as a Christian, I require recorded eyewitness accounts from multiple sources. I don't have enough faith to base my eternity off a YouTube video.

As a second tier of a response, ask, "If for argument's sake there were a person who lived one thousand years ago named David Mills, and he had four kids, and his wife's name was Kerry, and he loved deer hunting and was in the military, can you explain to me how that would *disprove* my existence?" There's no logical refutation of Jesus by saying there's an earlier myth that is similar. Just check out the book called *The Wreck of the Titan* by Morgan Robertson about a British ship that hits an iceberg and sinks in the North Atlantic in April and does not have enough lifeboats for its passengers. This book was published in 1898—fourteen years before the *Titanic* sank. And it doesn't disprove the *Titanic*.

3. YOU DON'T REALLY BELIEVE THOSE FAIRY TALES IN THE BIBLE, DO YOU?

This one used to scare me because I didn't want to look naïve or ridiculous. It does carry some rhetorical weight. The question behind the query here is, "Do you believe *everything* in the Bible?" I'm going to give you two responses to this, and you can pick one based on who's asking.

Keep in mind the continuum (truth → God → miracles → Jesus's resurrection) and find out where they are by asking, "Do you believe that miracles are possible?" If they say yes, then I will simply agree and say, "Me too, and the Old Testament chronicles some of those miracles." If they say no, then you simply back up on the continuum and ask them if they believe there's a God. If they say yes, then it ends there, for if God exists, then miracles are possible. If they say no, then ask them *if there was ever a time in their life when they did believe in God.* If so, then ask them what has changed their mind. Often, you find that it was something bad, a tragedy perhaps, or maybe it was a skeptical professor. Either way, they are now telling you what they believe and why. This takes some pressure off you. You're not trying to prove the story of Noah, and you're learning how to better talk to them about God.

The other response is more geared toward a sincere Christian who is genuinely asking whether you think these events are literal. To this, I will respond that I really don't know and that there are clearly many parts of the Bible that are not meant to be taken literally—for example,

- Job 38:4 (the earth does not have a literal foundation),
- 1 Samuel 2:8 (the earth is not literally sitting on pillars),
- John 6:35 (Jesus was not literally made of bread),
- Matthew 13:31 (The mustard seed is not literally the smallest of all seeds).

You get the idea. The Bible is full of parables, metaphors, and figures of speech (like sunrise—even though the sun does not literally rise). So, since we all concede that *these* items are figurative, I have no problem knowing that other parts may be figurative as well. I'm OK with that. Don't let a figure of speech derail your faith in the resurrection.

4. CHRISTIANS JUST CHERRY-PICK THE PARTS OF THE BIBLE THEY LIKE

Anytime a Christian speaks out against a sin, expect this one to come up. It comes up regularly when people discuss what the Bible says about homosexuality (more on this on statement 16). You may hear your son or daughter say, "Well, the Bible also says not to wear clothing made of two different fabrics, and it says to stone anyone caught in adultery, and I don't see you following those commands! You just pick out the ones you like, but you ignore the inconvenient ones."

This is more of a general complaint against Christians than an actual argument against God. But like I've said earlier, when fielding questions, don't expect to get a well-reasoned, logical argument from them.

Most of what people have to offer is emotional or volitional. And it probably won't have anything to do with whether Christianity is true. It will have to do with whether they like Christians or not.

Logically speaking, Christians can be hypocrites and cherry pickers, and Christianity can still be true. But rather than engage them in that logic, let's address their accusation. It's very easy.

"Oh, it sounds like you're referencing the laws from the Jewish Torah. I'm not Jewish. I'm a Christian, so I follow Jesus and the new covenant."[14] It's that easy.

Now, if you want to go deeper, you can explain the difference between civic, ceremonial, and moral laws and how the civic and ceremonial laws were prescribed for a certain people in a certain time (like making a right turn on a red light or standing up when the bride walks down the aisle), while moral laws are universally applied (like theft, murder, rape, etc.). But, honestly, I would go with the first answer. This is why it's so important to understand what Christians believe and remember tactic 1: avoid taking the Old Testament bait.

Here are a few verses to help us see this point I'm making in scripture:

⚒ "But now we are released from the law, having died to that which held us captive, so that we serve in the new way of the Spirit and not in the old way of the written code" (Rom 7:6).

⚒ "But as it is, Christ has obtained a ministry that is as much more excellent than the old as the covenant he mediates is better, since it is enacted on better promises" (Heb 8:6).

⚒ "In speaking of a new covenant, he makes the first one obsolete. And what is becoming obsolete and growing old is ready to vanish away" (Heb 8:13).

⚒ "Therefore, he is the mediator of a new covenant, so that those who are called may receive the promised eternal inheritance, since a death has occurred that redeems them from the transgressions committed under the first covenant" (Heb 9:15).

⚒ "For sin will have no dominion over you, since you are not under law but under grace" (Rom 6:14).

Therefore, keep bringing it back to the New Testament—the new covenant. We are not under the Old Testament. We don't have to live by it or explain it or pledge allegiance to it. And when you're sharing Christianity with someone, you will do well to know what you believe and why you believe it and stick to the gospel message—the good news of Jesus dying to pay for our sins and his resurrection!

Note: All the commands you and I need to keep are found in the New Testament. This includes nine of the Ten Commandments. The one not found in the NT is keeping the Sabbath. (And the NT speaks loudly enough against homosexuality that you don't need to reference the OT. See 1 Cor 6:9–11, Rom 1:24–28, 1 Tm 1:8–11, Jude 1:7, Mt 19:4–6.)

5. WE'RE BOTH ATHEISTS WHEN IT COMES TO 99 PERCENT OF ALL GODS

"We're both atheists when it comes to Zeus, Ra, Allah, and Neptune. You're already an atheist when it comes to 99 percent of all the gods. I just take it one step further. I just don't believe in one god more than you." This line can sound witty and smart when Ricky Gervais says it to Stephen Colbert or when Dawkins and Hitchens use it in debates, but it's actually completely hollow. It's merely the definition of an atheist and a Christian. An atheist believes in no God, and a Christian believes in one God.

A married man is a bachelor when it comes to 99 percent of all the women in the world. But being married to just one woman means you're not a bachelor at all. So, whether we're talking about having a wife or believing in God, the difference between none and one makes all the difference in the world.

6. JESUS NEVER EVEN CLAIMED TO BE GOD

Some people think that the deity of Jesus was a later invention by the authors of the New Testament. Before you launch into refuting them with overwhelming evidence for the deity of Jesus, this is a great time to use the tactic "How did you come to that conclusion?" This allows them to demonstrate what evidence they have for their position. Maybe they've read a book or heard a podcast. Ask them if they've considered the arguments *against* that book or podcast.

Someone who says, "Jesus never even claimed to be God," needs to be asked, "Have you read the New Testament?" It's amazing how many people have an opinion on the most famous person who has ever lived on this planet without even reading the book about him! Saying Jesus didn't claim to be God is like saying Clark Kent never even claimed to be Superman. Seriously? Have you even seen the movie? Everyone, whether atheist, Muslim, or Jew, owes it to themselves to at least read the gospel of John and Paul's letter to the Philippians.

Muslims famously use this argument. They cite Mark 10:17–22, where a young man calls Jesus "good teacher," and Jesus replies, "Why do you call me good? No one is good except for God." Notice that Jesus is not denying that he is good or that he is God. Rather, he is challenging the young man to consider that goodness does not come from our works but rather from God.

The other go-to verse of Muslims and atheists is Matthew 24:36. "But of that day and hour no one knows, not even the angels of heaven, nor the Son, but the Father alone."

The answer is simple. Jesus is both God and man (John 1:1, 14; 20:28; and Col 2:9, "For in Christ all the fullness of the Deity lives in bodily form"), and during his ministry in Jerusalem, he was cooperating with the limitations of being a man. As a man, Jesus walked and talked. As God, he was worshipped (Mt 14:33; 28:9; Heb 1:6), prayed to (1 Cor 1:2), etc. This is called the Hypostatic Union.

During his earthly ministry, he moved in the power of the Holy Spirit and did his miracles by the Holy Spirit and not by his own divine power. This is because he was made for a little while lower than the angels (Heb 2:9) and had emptied himself and taken on the form of a man (Phil 2:7).[15]

While on the earth, Jesus emptied himself of his power. He ate, slept, cried, and was executed. So, while he was on the earth, Jesus was self-limited on some of his knowledge and power.

But these two slightly perplexing verses should not be isolated from the dozens of verses that are crystal clear. Anytime we find a passage in the Bible that is confusing, we should interpret it in light of those sections that are clarifying.[16] Here are a few verses that show us that Jesus is, in fact, God: Matthew 16:13–20, 27:54, 28:19 (Trinity); Mark 14:61–64, 15:38–39; Luke 2:49, 4:17–21; John 4:25–26, 5:18, 6:38–40, 8:23–29, 8:42, 8:58 (in conjunction with Exodus 3:14), 10:30, 10:33, 14:6, 14:9, 16:28, 17:5, 18:5–6, 20:28–29; Colossians 2:9; 1 Timothy 3:16; Titus 2:13; Hebrews 1:5–8; Revelation 1:1, 1:8, 1:17–18.

Then there's the fact that Jesus did things only God can do, such as forgive sins (Is 43:25), allow people to worship him (John 9:35–38), refer to himself as I Am (Mk 14:62 in conjunction with Dn 7:13–14), say he is the Lord of the Sabbath (Mt 12:8), and change the Ten Commandments (Mt 5:21–28).

Philippians 2:5–11 is an outstanding explanation of who Jesus is in relationship to God. Go read it right now.

Additionally, a good question to ask is, "Why did the Jewish leaders demand that Jesus be crucified?" The answer, of course, is that Jesus was claiming to be God, which the Jews considered blasphemy (a crime punishable by death). This was why the Romans found no crime to convict Jesus of. So, anyone who says Jesus doesn't claim to be God must then come up with some new reason for the Jews demanding that Jesus be crucified.

7. RELIGION IS RESPONSIBLE FOR MOST OF THE WARS AND ATROCITIES

This is a fashionable thing for people like Bill Maher to say because it makes them sound like a noble peace-maker who wants nothing to do with wars or atrocities. There's just one small problem with this claim—it is totally false.

Begin your reply with tactic 3, "How did you come to that conclusion?" It's surprising how the same people who demand mountains of evidence from Christians will turn right around and believe the first thing they hear on television that supports atheism. Ask them what percentage of all wars were caused by religion. Then relax while listening to the crickets.

According to the *Encyclopedia of Wars*, of the 1,763 wars fought in the last five thousand years, only 123 (less than 7 percent) were motivated by religion.[17] In fact, the biggest mass murderers in all human history—Lenin, Stalin, Khrushchev, Hitler, Mao, and Pol Pot—killed an estimated 120 million people, and they were all atheists! (Don't let anyone try to tell you Hitler was Catholic. If you read his writings, you know he despised Jesus—who was a Jew!) Note: These atheistic mass murderers were all in the latest century, which refutes the notion that the world is improving.

This means that if you're going to choose your worldview based on who has committed the most wars and atrocities, then you should literally choose anything other than atheism. As Greg Koukl says, "The greatest evil has not come from people zealous for God. It has come from people who are convinced there is no God they must answer to."[18]

Furthermore, even if this claim actually were true, that still wouldn't disprove Christianity. It would just demonstrate that people do bad things, which the Bible already tells us is the case, and that's why we need a Savior.

Last, why would an atheist think that murder is wrong? And what makes something an atrocity exactly? In the worldview of survival of the fittest and natural selection, the atheist has no foundation from which they can condemn war, mass murder, and atrocities. If we are all just animals, then why shouldn't the stronger take whatever they want from the weaker? Where have they come up with this objective moral law (see appendix 1, "Moral Law")? It is only within a worldview that believes humans have intrinsic value that we ought not murder.

8. THE BIBLE IS FULL OF ERRORS AND CONTRADICTIONS

The Bible has been translated so many times that no one knows what the original even says. Like the game of telephone, where you whisper something to one person, and they whisper it to another, by the time it's gone around the room, it's completely different.

Once again, start your reply by asking, "How did you come to that conclusion?" Have you studied the transmission of the early manuscripts?

News flash! The one who makes the claim must provide the evidence.

When your friend or family member says the Bible is full of errors, they have just made a truth claim. They have asserted something to be true, and it is not our job to refute them until they have first supported their own claim. So, ask them to provide their supporting material. It is something most of them have never even considered since they're probably parroting a statement they have heard someone else say.

Perhaps they're unaware that the Bible hasn't been transmitted by whispering it one time to a person like the telephone game. It has been written down, and copies have been made, widely distributed, and translated into other languages and circulated around the Mediterranean region and beyond. We have about twenty-six thousand pieces of early manuscripts (thousands more than any other piece of historical writing) that we can still go back to and look at to make sure that today's translations are still accurate.

A better analogy than the telephone game is copying and distributing one hundred copies of your grand-ma's best cookie recipe, and those one hundred people each copy it one hundred times also. So, if one of those 10,000 copies says "tablespoon of vanilla," and the other 9,999 say "teaspoon of vanilla," we can easily determine that scribe has made an error because we have so many texts to compare it with. We can also go back to the original one hundred copies you have made and see what it says. And, if years later, one recipe starts adding nuts, it will be easy to demonstrate that someone has added their own words to that recipe that are not in the originals.

Note: If you were to round up all ten thousand copies of the recipe and burn them all except for the one you liked best, then no one would ever be able to know what the original said. And that was exactly what happened with the Koran. Shortly before being assassinated in AD 656, Caliph Uthman collected and burned all variant texts of the Koran.[19] (He also rearranged the Koran from longest chapters to shortest, so it is not in any chronological or logical order.) So, Islam does not have the variants, numbers of manuscripts, or historicity that the New Testament enjoys.

In fact, the New Testament has an "embarrassment of riches," according to Dan Wallace, founder of the Center for the Study of New Testament Manuscripts (CSNTM). The CSNTM has a digital catalogue of each piece of papyrus digitally scanned for preservation. (Check it out at CSNTM.org.)

A fantastic response when someone asserts that the Bible is "full of contradictions and errors" is to politely ask them, "Can you tell me exactly which contradictions or errors are bothering you?"

Bart Ehrman is the professor of religious studies at the University of North Carolina at Chapel Hill. He completed his MDiv and PhD at Princeton Seminary and has served as president of the Southeast Region of the Society of Biblical Literature and chair of the New Testament textual criticism section of the society. Ehrman is also an outspoken atheist who has taken on numerous Christians in debate.

So, if you want to hear the absolute best, A-game material that atheists have on the topic of errors and contradictions in the Bible, you look to Bart Ehrman. And you know what you find? Nothing. With great flourish and theatrics, Ehrman points out that we don't know how many women were at the empty tomb. He says the gospel accounts are different, and if we can't know this detail for sure, then how can we know any of it for sure?

I don't know about you, but hearing that gives me great confidence in the reliability of the New Testament. That's the best they've got? Now, the gospel of Matthew names two women, both named Mary, who were at the tomb (28:1). The gospel of Mark names both Marys and tells us there was also a woman named Salome with them (16:1). In Luke's gospel, he names the two Marys, plus Joanna "and the others with them" (24:10). And in John 20:1–2, he names one

ANSWERING THE HARD STUFF

of the Marys who says, "*We* don't know where they have put him" (italics added). So, we know that there were at least four women (Mary Magdalene, Mary the mother of James, Salome, and Joanna), but there could've been several more. No account in the gospels says that their list is complete. No one is saying there were *only* two Marys or *only* three women. It's quite possible that there was a very large group of women.

This is not a contradiction. This is a difference. A contradiction would be if one account said Joanna was *not* there, and another account said Joanna *was* there. *That's* a contradiction.

News flash! Only made-up stories state all of the exact same details. When a homicide detective interviews four different people who all say the exact same thing, word for word, the detective knows that they have colluded together beforehand, and they are not telling the truth.[20]

The gospel accounts agree on all major points. But they give the stories from different perspectives, and some record the events thematically, others chronologically, and still others by importance to them. Even Bart Ehrman admits that none of the differences in the gospel accounts have to do with the central elements of Jesus's life, death, and resurrection claim.

When it comes to "errors" in the New Testament, they can really spin that one too. Often, you will hear a number of errors, such as two hundred thousand, in the New Testament. Ehrman likes to say that there are more errors in the New Testament than there are total words! That sounds really bad, right? Well, these "errors" are things like spelling. One writer says "Petra," one says "Peter," and another says "Simon Peter." Which is it? That counts as three variants. I think you're starting to get the picture.

If you want to go deeper on this topic, I recommend reading *I Don't Have Enough Faith to Be an Atheist* by Turek or *Cold-Case Christianity* by Wallace. But suffice it to say, there are no errors or contradictions in the New Testament, merely differences and variants.

I want to just touch briefly on some other wacky conspiracy theories out there, such as the New Testament was written hundreds of years after Jesus lived, or it was all made up at the Council of Nicaea. No serious scholar believes this. It's in Hollywood movies and YouTube videos, so just use tactic 3 and ask them for their evidence. We, as Christians, actually have evidence for what we believe. So, ask them for their evidence for what they believe.

The book of Acts was written before AD 70, when the temple was destroyed. And Luke wrote his gospel before he wrote Acts. So, the book of Luke was earlier than Acts. And Luke used the gospel of Mark as a reference, so we know that Mark came even earlier. So, we have good evidence that much of the NT was written quite early (AD 50–60). (To help put this into perspective, the only *two* written accounts we have of Alexander the Great were written over four hundred years after he died!) And the creeds given in 1 Corinthians 15 and in Philippians 2 are even earlier than the gospels. Some scholars put those creeds in the AD 30s–40s.[21] So we know that within ten to twenty years of Jesus's resurrection, creeds had been written, circulated around the region, and translated into numerous languages even before Paul codified them in his letters.

There are more manuscripts from more writers from an earlier date for the life, death, and resurrection of Jesus than we have for the life of Julius Caesar (or any other person in ancient history)! And the life, death, and resurrection claims by the followers of Jesus can be verified by nonbiblical historians like Tacitus, Josephus, Pliny the Younger, and Suetonius! So, without even referencing the Bible, we know that there was a man named Jesus who was from Nazareth and lived in the first century who people claimed did miracles, that he was executed by the Romans on a cross, and whose followers claimed rose from the dead!

9. THE GOD OF THE OLD TESTAMENT IS A MONSTER!

In his book *The God Delusion*, Richard Dawkins complains, "The God of the Old Testament is arguably the most unpleasant character in all fiction: jealous and proud of it; a petty, unjust, unforgiving control-freak; a vindictive, bloodthirsty ethnic cleanser; a misogynistic, homophobic, racist, infanticidal, genocidal, filicidal, pestilential, megalomaniacal, sadomasochistic, capriciously malevolent bully."[22]Statements like this are derived from God commanding the Israelites to annihilate the Canaanites and the Philistines or from God telling Abraham to sacrifice his son Isaac. I'm not sure what exactly this argument is meant to prove. It is incoherent to argue that you don't approve of someone, *and* you don't believe they exist.

If your teenager is turning away from Christianity because they think God is a monster, ask them, "Are you saying God does not exist, *and* you don't like him?" Logically speaking, if the Bible is fiction, then God cannot be a monster. And if the Bible is true, then, well, he's God.

We might not understand God, but then again, if our human minds could fully understand all the thoughts of God, then he wouldn't be much of a God. So, it's OK to not understand him. It's even OK to be mad at him. (Many of the Psalms are King David's anger over not understanding God.) A lot of people are mad at God. Hating God isn't evidence that he does not exist.

If you take an art class, is it wrong to go around the room destroying all the other students' paintings? Of course, it is. What about your own painting? If you don't like how it looks, is there anything wrong with painting over your own canvas in white paint and just starting over? Why is messing up your painting acceptable, but it's not acceptable to mess up anyone else's? The answer is obvious—because it's *your* painting.

Well, God is the artist of all creation, and as the Creator, it is not wrong for him to erase his own work and start over. He is the Author of life, and when we say God is a moral monster, we are judging him by our standards.

Just as a surgeon may remove someone's arm to save their life, so God may remove one person or group of persons for a greater good. He sees a bigger picture than we're able to.

It might also help provide a bit of historical context on what exactly the Canaanites were doing. They were sacrificing their living infant babies by laying them in the red-hot iron arms of their idol Moloch. God had enough of this evil, and he used the Israelites to go put an end to it.

People often wish that, if God existed, he would stop evil from happening. Well, in the Old Testament we have a story of God doing just that. God saw people doing unspeakable evil, burning their babies alive, and he stopped it. So, do we want God to stop evil so we can call him a monster, or do you want him to let it happen so we can wonder where he is?

10. SCIENCE HAS ALREADY DISPROVED GOD

Remember: it is not your job to refute their claim that science has disproved God; rather, it is their job to support it. So, when someone says, "Science has disproved God," just ask them to explain how exactly.

What they will probably get down to eventually is Darwinian evolution. That is more than likely where their claim about science is headed. When this happens, do not get into a debate about finches or peppered moths or the age of the universe. Just ask them, "What caused the big bang?" What exactly *caused* it? And where did *it* come from?

Thanks to Edwin Hubble, we have known since 1929 that the universe has a beginning. It is not eternal. Something went "bang" an awfully long time ago, and the universe has been expanding ever since.

So, there are only two options on the table:

1. Everything came from nothing. This would require tons of unscientific, unsupported, blind faith to believe that, once upon a time, there was *nothing*, and then—poof!—there was something.

2. In the beginning, God created the heavens and the earth.

It has nothing to do with macroevolution or common ancestry. For the sake of expediency, I'll allow them all that. But where did that primordial soup come from?

You see, if you're an atheist, then you believe in a much bigger miracle than anything in the Bible. You believe that humpback whales, hummingbirds, and Labrador retrievers have all come into existence from *nothing*. That's worse than magic. At least with magic, you have a hat and a magician. Atheists are claiming that the entire stage and theater magically appeared out of thin air.[23]

News flash! Thousands of scientists at top universities disagree with Darwinism. Signatories of the "Scientific Dissent from Darwinism" hold doctorates in biological sciences, physics, chemistry, mathematics, medicine, computer science, and related disciplines from such institutions as Oxford, Cambridge, Harvard, Dartmouth, Rutgers, University of Chicago, Stanford, and University of California at Berkeley. They've all signed the following statement:

> We are skeptical of claims for the ability of random mutation and natural selection to account for the complexity of life. Careful examination of the evidence for Darwinian theory should be encouraged.

Yet many of our kids are not aware of this. They've been told that all scientists agree. That's simply not true. You can view the entire list of scientists at www. dissentfromdarwin.org.

We're all still waiting to hear how the field of science, which was founded by Christians (Francis Bacon, Copernicus, Galileo, Newton, Faraday), has disproved God's existence. Furthermore, it's only possible to practice science if we live in an orderly universe with unchanging laws. If things were actually random, then the results of one experiment would be different the next day, and an unguided, ungoverned, random universe of chaos would be unknowable and very unscientific.

Learning how the world works and figuring out all its intricate systems doesn't mean we no longer need a creator. Some people mistakenly think that we only invoke a God when we don't know how something works. Like before humans understood lightning, they thought God was mad and throwing lightning bolts. And as we gain more knowledge of how things work, we may eventually not need a God at all. This is called the "God of the gaps" theory.

But we're not invoking God because of things we *don't* understand. We're invoking God because of what we *do* understand—like DNA, for instance. The more we learn about it, the more it points to a Designer. DNA is digitally encoded information. Have you ever seen information come from nothing? Books have authors, paintings have artists, buildings have engineers, and software has a programmer. The information in your DNA is enough to fill a library![24] Where has that come from? It points to a Designer. Legendary atheist Antony Flew actually changed his mind and believed in God based on the evidence for a Creator in human DNA[25] (more on this in appendix 1).

Scientists who think that because of their knowledge of the universe, they don't need God to explain it is like a mechanic who knows so much about cars that he starts to doubt the existence of Henry Ford. Hey, that's great that you know so much about how cars work, but the whole thing still had to be designed by someone.

Last, if a person believes that their own mind was created through an unguided, unintelligent process of random mutations, then why would they trust their own thoughts? You wouldn't trust a computer that has been randomly assembled through an unguided, undesigned process to do your taxes, would you?[26]

Science can never disprove God because science is the study of the natural world. God, by definition is supernatural; therefore, he is outside the realm of science.

Remember: this objection falls into bucket 3, scientism. Refer back to that for more ways to respond.

11. A LOT OF FANATICS WILL DIE FOR THEIR FAITH; THAT DOESN'T PROVE THEY'RE TELLING THE TRUTH

"Just because a person dies for what they believe in doesn't make it true. Look at the Islamic terrorists of 9/11. They were all willing to die for their beliefs. Does that make Islam true?" If you try telling a family member that the apostles' willingness to die for their belief in the resurrection is good evidence that it's true, you may hear them say this response.

The difference they need to understand is that while this demonstrates that people will die for what they believe to be true, it does *not* indicate that people will die for something they have made up and know to be false. So, their analogy actually highlights the fact that the apostles died for what *they believed* to be true. They did not make up a lie that would get them dipped in boiling oil, crucified upside down, or sawed in half. They died because they believed it is true. And unlike today's terrorists, the apostles were *the* firsthand eyewitnesses.

Today's Islamic terrorists are indeed dying for what they believe to be true based on what they've been *taught.* But the disciples of Jesus were believing what they had *seen.*

12. YOU'RE ONLY A CHRISTIAN BECAUSE YOU WERE BORN IN AMERICA (OR YOUR PARENTS ARE CHRISTIAN)

"If you were born in ancient Greece, you'd probably worship Zeus. And if you were born in Saudi Arabia, you'd probably be Muslim. So, the only reason why you're a Christian is that you were born here and now." This is called a genetic fallacy, which is a flawed assumption that something is true or false based on where you learned it. If your third-grade teacher turns out to be a convicted felon, that does not mean that all the multiplication tables they taught you are wrong. Whether something is true or false has nothing to do with where you live, when you were born, or what your parents believe.

TACTIC 4—ALWAYS RESPOND WITH A QUESTION

Ask the person if they were born in America. If they say yes and they are not a Christian, then they are living proof that their own theory is flawed. Ask them if they believe everything just as their parents do. They will say no. And you can inform them that neither do you.

It's also good to remind people that there are an estimated two hundred million Christians in China, that there are more pastors in Africa than in America, that South Korea now sends missionaries to America, and that Christianity originated in the Middle East.

To be honest, it is indeed a privilege to have been born in twentieth-century America. And that is probably the reason *why* we know many of the things that we know. I am indeed more fortunate than someone born in a third-world country. That's why we have a burden to share what we've learned with people. So, we should leverage the benefit of our exceptional upbringing to seek truth as much as possible.

Being born into a Christian family or living in America may be the reason that we have learned the truth, but that has nothing to do with its veracity. A person can just as easily say to me, "The only reason you learned about Shakespeare is that you went to school in the Western Hemisphere." They may be correct, but that doesn't disprove Shakespeare.

TACTIC 5—GET THEM TO ASK YOU FOR THE EVIDENCE

Try saying, "I'm only a Christian because of the evidence." Then let there be a silent pause.

When they ask you, "What evidence?" then you have just accomplished something amazing. They have just asked you to give them the gospel! Now, you're not being preachy; you're just answering their question. (See appendix 2 for the evidence that Christianity is true.)

13. HOW COULD A GOD ALLOW ALL THIS SUFFERING AND EVIL IN THE WORLD?

The atheists' argument goes like this:

1. An all-powerful God could stop evil.

2. An all-loving God would stop evil.

3. There is evil in the world.

4. Therefore, an all-powerful, all-loving God does not exist.

The flaw in this argument is premise 1 and 2. Premise 1 is not true in a world where God has given people free will. Yes, God could have created a world without evil, but then it would also be a world without love because you cannot love unless you also have the free will to choose to hate. Premise 2 assumes God does not have a reason for allowing pain and suffering that may bring about a greater good. It's logically possible that if God exists, then we little humans may not fully grasp his overarching, sovereign plan.[27]

As a parent, I have allowed my little children to be stuck with needles. I've even been the one to take them into the room and hold them on my lap while it happens. I've understood that the needle is a vaccine that will bring about a greater good. So, I've allowed some temporary pain and suffering in their life. As the children of God, we won't always know God's plan or be able to comprehend why bad things are happening. But we can trust that he is sovereign and that a greater good will come from it.

A good question to ask in return is "What do you mean by evil?" This will cause them to stop and think for a person cannot ask, "How could a loving God allow evil in the world?" unless they admit that there is an objective standard of good and evil. And this leads once again to the moral argument *for* the existence of God (see appendix 1). You want to help them realize that without God, they cannot know good from evil.

Richard Dawkins is at least being a consistent atheist when he says, "The universe we observe has precisely the properties we should expect if there is, at bottom, no design, no purpose, no evil, no good, nothing but blind, pitiless indifference."[28] He gets it. In an atheistic worldview, there is no such thing as evil. There's just "pitiless indifference." If you firmly believe there are *no* objective rules in basketball, then you *don't* get to cry foul when something happens that you don't like. Calling foul implicitly confirms that rules exist, and all rules have a rule giver.

Asking them to define what they mean by evil will help them come to terms with a few key facts that up until now they may have never considered:

1. When they say "evil," they are implying that there is a universal, objective standard of right and wrong, of good and evil.

2. If good and evil are objectively real and not just a matter of my opinion, then where has this objective moral law come from?

3. If you have your truth and I have my truth, then you can't call a kidnapper or a racist or Hitler evil.

At this point, some people will admit that there is actual right and wrong but that they just know what's right in their heart; they don't need the Bible to tell them that murder is wrong.

That's true. Paul tells us that we know good from evil because God has written these laws in the heart of man (Rom 2:15). We are made in God's image, and we live in his universe whether we acknowledge him or not. The fact that we know right from wrong makes sense in a Christian worldview, but it makes zero sense if we are here by survival of the fittest and natural selection. Hitler was a survivor. The rapist is the fittest and strongest. Why shouldn't the stronger, fitter, smarter person with the most weapons just take what they want? In the worldview of Darwinian evolution and atheism, there is no way to objectively condemn these actions. It's all a relative opinion.

There is evil in this world because God has created us with free will. And many people use that free will to choose to go against God. They choose evil. We've all chosen evil, haven't we? We've all lied, stolen, cheated, and lusted. So we're all evil.

However, there cannot be evil unless there is good. There cannot be good unless there is an objective standard outside ourselves applicable for all people everywhere. We call that standard God. Sure, people can *be* good without God, and they can *know* good without acknowledging God, but they cannot *define* good apart from God.

It has been said that "evil doesn't disprove God any more than shadows disprove the sun." It's because of the sun that we can see shadows at all.

So, your son or daughter cannot logically complain about evil without acknowledging that a universal moral standard of right and wrong is known in the hearts of all people, in every nation, and in every period. Where has that universal knowledge come from?

This brings us to one more point about evil. God did not create evil. Evil is simply the absence of good.

God did not create darkness either. God created light. Darkness is the absence of light, and evil is the absence of good.

14. WHY DO BAD THINGS HAPPEN TO GOOD PEOPLE?

This question is really another way of asking question 13 except that it implies that there are *good* people, which makes this question a great opener for giving the gospel. Just ask them, "Do you think you're a good person?" Most people think they are. I love how Ray Comfort uses these questions:

- Have you ever told a lie?
- What do you call someone who tells a lie?
- Have you ever stolen anything? Even time from your employer?
- What do you call someone who steals?
- Have you ever looked lustfully at someone you aren't married to?

✖ Jesus said if you commit adultery in your heart, then you're guilty of it.

✖ So, by your own admission, you're a liar, thief, and an adulterer at heart.

You see, no one is good but God (Mk 10:18).

The New Testament gives us hope that evil people will be punished and people who do good will be rewarded. Unlike atheism, Christianity offers hope of a final accounting of all our actions at the final judgment. So, we can rest assured that ultimate justice will be served.

There has only been one occurrence in human history of bad things happening to a good person, and his name is Jesus.

15. WHY DOES GOD SEND PEOPLE TO HELL FOR NOT BELIEVING IN HIM?

That's like asking why a judge would send people to jail just because they can't post bail. The judge sends people to jail because *they have broken the law*. It's the crime that causes people to go to jail. The fact that they could not post bail is unfortunate, but it's not what landed them in jail.

Likewise, God does *not* send people to hell because they don't believe in him. It's our moral crimes (called sins) that condemn us all to hell. That's the bad news. The good news is that our bail has been posted for us already. Jesus posted our bail when he died on the cross. That was him paying the penalty for our sins. All we need to do is accept that payment!

16. "PROGRESSIVE CHRISTIANITY" AND DECONSTRUCTING YOUR FAITH

One of the latest trends in Christianity is to "deconvert" or deconstruct one's faith. This is unusually common among celebrity Christian singers and popular mega pastors for some reason. (Hey, even God had trouble with his musicians.) Of course, many celebrity Christians have likely never truly been born again in the first place but rather were in it for their celebrity status. Some of these include DC Talk's Kevin Max, Hawk Nelson's Jon Steingard, and former pastor and best-selling author Joshua Harris. "Exvangelical" is how Kevin Max describes himself now. From Christian worship band Hillsong United, Marty Sampson now says he is no longer a Christian either. And famous author and pastor's wife Jen Hatmaker has followed suit in abandoning Christianity and the church, even filing for divorce along the way.

All these deconversion stories and the title "progressive Christianity" all have one thing in common: an unwillingness to label anything as a sin. Behind every article on a celebrity deconversion is a message of not wanting to judge people and not wanting to condemn sexual behaviors that the Bible calls detestable. It's really just a desire to follow the LGBTQ movement instead of following Jesus. It's really that simple.

Society is going one way, the Bible stands steadfast in the opposite direction, and the people choose social acceptance over the Word of God, period. The rest is just smoke and lights, but the root of it is really just that simple.

So, when you're having a conversation with a family member on this topic, just use the same message from pluralism (p. 8) and ask them, "What does the New Testament say about this?" Jesus says marriage is between one man and one woman (Mt 19:4–6). Romans 1:26–27 calls homosexual sex indecent and unnatural. First Corinthians 6:9–11 says, "Or do you not know that wrongdoers will not inherit the kingdom of God? Do not be deceived: Neither the sexually immoral nor idolaters nor adulterers nor men who have sex with men nor thieves nor the greedy nor drunkards nor slanderers nor swindlers will inherit the kingdom of God. And that is what some of you were. But you were washed, you were sanctified, you were justified in the name of the Lord Jesus Christ and by the Spirit of our God." And 1 Timothy 1:9–10 tells us, "We also know that the law is made not for the righteous but for lawbreakers and rebels, the ungodly and sinful, the unholy and irreligious, for those who kill their fathers or mothers, for murderers, for the sexually immoral, for those practicing homosexuality, for slave traders and liars and perjurers—and for whatever else is contrary to the sound doctrine."

Clearly, we do not need to argue with anyone. We simply point them toward the New Testament, and then it's up to them to either accept or reject it. (Notice that I use only NT verses. See statement 4, "Christians Just Cherry-Pick the Parts of the Bible They Like.")

There's nothing new or progressive about rejecting the Word of God when it doesn't fit with culture. It's simply a matter of who is in charge—you or God?

17. CHRISTIANS ARE NOT SUPPOSED TO JUDGE

Anytime a Christian takes a stand on an issue (abortion, homosexuality, capital punishment, etc.), they are inevitably going to hear the assertion "You're not supposed to judge others" or "The Bible says not to judge." This is intended to silence the Christians—or the Bible actually. Society doesn't want to be told that what they're doing is wrong or immoral or sinful, so they use this "don't judge" phrase to silence the convicting Word of God. That's what's going on, and it's important that we understand that. The person saying this is not serious about obeying the Bible and its position on judgment. If you want to find that out for yourself, just ask them, "So, you're saying we should follow everything that the Bible says?" Of course, they will say no. (Hmmm, are they just cherry-picking the parts of the Bible that they like?)

Actually, the Bible does *not* tell us not to judge others; the Bible teaches us *how* to judge others. Matthew 7:1–3 is the go-to reference for this conversation, and it reads, "Do not judge, or you too will be judged. For in the same way you judge others, you will be judged, and with the measure you use, it will be measured to you. Why do you look at the speck of sawdust in your brother's eye and pay no attention to the plank in your own eye?"

What this passage teaches is to not judge hypocritically. It's saying to not hold others to a different standard from what we hold ourselves and to make sure that we clean up our own lives before we try to fix those of others.

And if you think about this concept for more than two seconds, you'll see how imperative it is that we, as Christians, judge the actions of others. First Thessalonians 5:22 says, "Reject every kind of evil." How can we reject evil if we don't use our judgment to know what is evil and what is good? Romans 12:2 tells us "to test and approve what is the good, pleasing, and perfect will of God." This also requires us to make judgments of what is right. First Corinthians 6:18 tells us to "run from sexual sin." Again, this literally requires Christians to judge.

Further, we're told to pray for wisdom (Jas 1) so that we can discern the will of God. The entire purpose of wisdom and discernment is to judge what is right and what is wrong. The Christian life is about judging properly, whether it's our own actions (Jas 4:17), those of our friends (Prv 12:26), or an argument or opinion that goes against God (2 Cor 10:5).

Furthermore, from a purely practical perspective, sound judgment is key to survival. We judge whom to hire as a babysitter, whom to marry, and whom to allow to be our pastor. We even judge the speed and distance of cars when crossing the street. Exercising sound judgment is essential to living wisely. Clearly, the Bible does not teach us not to judge other people at all, but rather it mandates that we judge ourselves by that same standard we apply to others.

HOW TO SHARE THE GOSPEL

A lot of Christians don't know what to do if the ball is lobbed slowly right down the middle of the plate. If your kid, neighbor, or coworker asks you, "How do I become a Christian?" that's a slow pitch right down the middle. And a good ambassador is ready with the answer so they can knock it out of the park.

TACTIC 6—LEAD WITH THE BAD NEWS

It's really difficult for people to grasp the good news (the gospel) until they first comprehend the bad news. "Jesus saves" or "Jesus is the answer" will fall on deaf ears in a culture as affluent as ours. "Jesus saves from what? Do I look like I need saving? Jesus is the answer? I didn't know there was a question. Have I found Jesus? I didn't know he was lost."

There are certainly many great ways to share the gospel. I'm not saying this is the exclusive, correct way to do it, but this works for me. I have learned this from Greg Koukl. It's easy to use and nonconfrontational, and it appeals to our sense of justice and love. Here is a great way to start:

Do you think people should be held accountable for their moral crimes? Yeah, me too. Have you ever committed any moral crimes? I know I have. I've stolen, lied, cheated, and hurt people.

So, we both agree that moral crimes ought to be punished. And we both agree that we've committed moral crimes. I would call that … bad news.

The apostle Paul wrote that no one is good enough to be in the presence of God. He says that God is so perfectly good that no sinner could even be near him. God is perfectly good, and we're all broken sinners.

Imagine a judge who is famous for being perfectly just. No criminal goes unpunished in his court. And this same judge is also known for being perfectly loving. He is the perfect picture of grace and love. Now, imagine that this judge's son is arrested for stealing from a store down the street. The son pleads guilty and stands before his father—the judge. Now, this judge has a dilemma. How can he remain perfectly just in the law and perfectly loving toward his child?

So, here's what the judge did. He found the young man guilty and sentenced him to the maximum fine according to the law. Then he stood up, took off his robe, walked down from his bench, and paid the fine for his son. That is perfect justice and perfect love. And that is exactly what God did for us when we stood before him, guilty of sins. He found us guilty and sentenced us to death (the apostle Paul wrote to the Romans that the penalty for sin is death). Then God took off his divine glory, took on human form named Jesus, lived a perfect life, and died as the ultimate payment for our sin. All we must do is accept that payment. Say, "God, I am a sinner, and I thank you for your payment on the cross on my behalf."

Can you imagine if that son stood there in the courtroom and said to the judge, "No thanks, I'll try to pay the fine myself," or "Maybe there are multiple paths to my redemption"? He'd be a fool. The payment is his life. And the God of the universe has already made that payment.

That's the story of Christianity. That's what we're guilty of. That's what God did in his justice and in his love. And God is also the owner of the store from which we stole.

The apostle John said that God loved the world so much that he gave his only Son, Jesus, to die on the cross for us and that anyone who puts their trust in Him will have eternal life. Now, that is the good news. Would you like to put your trust in Jesus right now?

Whenever you share your faith with someone, try to avoid all types of "Christianese." Don't say things like, "Ask Jesus into your heart," "Jesus wants to save you from your sins," or "The Bible says ..." Some of these phrases are so overused and cliché that they've lost their meaning in our culture. Try using fresh new language to capture attention in a new way—for instance,

Say this:	Instead of this:
Jesus of Nazareth	Jesus Christ
The apostle Paul wrote ...	The Bible says ...
Have you ever committed a moral crime?	Have you ever sinned?

Creator of the universe	God
Follower of Jesus	Christian
Put your trust in Jesus	Ask Jesus into your heart
The New Testament	The Bible
Luke's biography on Jesus	The Bible
Paul's letter to the Romans	The Bible
Jesus's death on a cross	The blood of Jesus

Make your message about a real person who lived in first-century Israel. He was born in Bethlehem, lived under the reign of Caesar Augustus, and was executed by the Romans on a wooden cross. This Jesus of Nazareth came back to life—as he predicted he would! And as you can imagine, this is the single most shocking, life-changing event in all human history! Those who knew Jesus and fished with him were all cowards when he got arrested and killed. But upon seeing him resurrected, they dedicated their lives to telling everyone they encountered about Jesus. They traveled on foot thousands of miles and were arrested, beaten, tortured, and killed, and not one of them ever recanted. No one changed their story!

Chuck Colson was Richard Nixon's chief of staff. In his book *Born Again*, Colson said, "I know the resurrection is a fact, and Watergate proved it to me. How? Because 12 men testified they had seen Jesus raised from the dead, then they proclaimed that truth for 40 years, never once denying it. Everyone was beaten, tortured, stoned, and put in prison. They would not have endured that if it weren't true. Watergate embroiled 12 of the most powerful men in the world— and they couldn't keep a lie for three weeks. You're telling me 12 apostles could keep a lie for 40 years? Absolutely impossible."[29]

TACTIC 7—RELAX; YOU DON'T HAVE TO HIT A HOME RUN, JUST TAKE A SWING

I grew up thinking that the way to give the gospel is to first ask people where they would go if they died tonight. And then you end with having them pray to ask Jesus into their hearts. This results in a high-pressure sales pitch that turns a lot of people off and leaves a lot of us feeling like we must not be particularly good Christians if we don't "close the deal."

Reading *Tactics* by Greg Koukl has helped take that pressure off. Not everyone can be a harvester. Some of us may be gardeners. We till the soil, we plant seeds, we water the ground, and maybe we harvest, or maybe we don't. It doesn't matter. We just do our part.

Try to put a pebble in people's shoes. You don't have to take them to the altar. Just give them something to think about, something to keep them awake at night.

FOUR POINTS TO REMEMBER

1. People don't reject God because of a lack of evidence. They reject God because they know he will interfere with their misconduct. But since they can't admit that at cocktail parties, they decide to pretend that it's because of a lack of evidence.

2. Atheists have more blind faith than Christians. They believe that the entire universe sprang into existence from nothing and that your DNA has no designer.

3. Most people aren't on a truth quest. They're on a happiness quest. They don't want a God to exist. So, ask people this: "If hypothetically Christianity were true, would you become a

Christian?" If they say no, then don't waste your time on them. Only invest in people who are seeking the truth.

4. Teach your kids what you believe and why. Talk to them about truth, God, miracles, Jesus's resurrection, and the New Testament manuscripts while driving around with them. Ask them to voice their questions over dinner. Share with them what you have learned while you're fishing. Role-play as an atheist and ask them hard questions while you're hiking. Memorize important Bible verses with them (see appendix 3). This is your job!

A sheepdog protects sheep from wolves, and as the spiritual leader in your family, your job is to be a sheepdog. Prepare them to respond to the wolves around them. Train them to articulate what they believe and why they believe it. Our kids are smart. They take Advanced Placement and honors classes, and they study molecular biology. So don't treat them like kindergartners when it comes to their faith.

Give your kids the gift of knowing what they believe and why so that they, too, will be great ambassadors!

APPENDIX 1
EVIDENCE FOR GOD

The first three arguments listed below are the *classical arguments for the existence of God*. A good ambassador is aware of the arguments that have existed for many years. When most people say, "There's no evidence for God," they are not even aware of these classical pieces of evidence. So, a good response is "Have you considered the classical arguments for God's existence?" (Notice that this uses tactic 4: always respond with a question.) We're not just launching into our argument but also asking them if they've considered them. This helps us gauge the level of knowledge they have on the subject and will likely lead to their asking us to share them.

Side note: The word *argument* used here does not mean a heated or angry exchange. When we say *argument*, we're referring to its definition as "a reason or set of reasons given with the aim of persuading others" (Dictionary.com).

Here are three classical arguments and one modern argument for the existence of God:

1. Kalam Cosmological Argument
   a. Whatever begins to exist has a cause.
   b. The universe began to exist.
   c. Therefore, the universe has a cause.

This argument is ancient and was first established within Islam. However, it has been adjusted and championed by William Lane Craig. The key component in the first premise is the word *begins*. There is only one thing that did not *begin* to exist—God, because he is eternal. Therefore, the skeptic cannot come back with "What caused God?" Nothing, for God did not *begin* to exist.

The second premise has been proved true by the works of Albert Einstein, who established that space, time, and matter all came to exist at the same time;

and by Edwin Hubble, who in 1929 established that the universe was expanding and thus had a beginning.

Therefore, some force, thing, person, or mind had to cause the universe to begin.

This is an airtight argument if the first two premises are true. The first is true by experience of the known and observable universe. There are, to date, no known examples of anything beginning to exist without a cause. And the second premise is proved through cosmology. Therefore, we can confidently conclude that someone or something caused our universe.

2. Teleological Argument
      d. Behind every complex design is a designer.
      e. The universe has a complex design.
      f. Therefore, the universe has a designer.

There is no debate among both atheists and theists that the universe, the earth, and life on earth display design. The most vocal atheist alive today, Richard Dawkins, admits: "Living objects ... look designed, they look overwhelmingly as though they're designed.

Biology is the study of complicated things which give the impression of having been designed for a purpose." Francis Crick, also an atheist, says, "Biologists must constantly keep in mind that what they see was not designed, but rather evolved."[30]

The theist responds that things look designed because they were in fact designed by a Creator. The teleological argument for God contends that one way we can validate the existence of a Creator is through the marks of intelligence and design that the universe and humankind exhibit.[31]

"Isaac Newton (1642–1727) implicitly confirmed the validity of the Teleological Argument when he marveled at the design of our solar system. He wrote, 'This most beautiful system of the sun, planets and comets, could only proceed from the counsel and dominion of an intelligent and powerful Being.'"[32]

According to astrophysicist Hugh Ross, if you adjusted, in either direction, by even the slightest bit the gravitational force, oxygen in the atmosphere, rotation or tilt of the earth, carbon dioxide level, or 117 other constants, then there would be no life on earth.[33] That is serious fine-tuning, the likes of which declare there's just no way it all happened by accident. As Turek points out, it takes a lot more faith to believe that this high level of fine-tuned design happened by chance than that there's a creator.

It is now quite common to hear atheists talk about the multiverse, which is a theory that says there might be an infinite number of universes out there. This theory has been concocted to rebut the teleological argument for the existence of God. However, there is zero evidence for it. It's a wild theory that requires a lot more faith to believe in than it takes to believe in God. If your friend proposes an infinite number of universes, just use tactic 3 and ask what evidence they have to support that theory.

3. Moral Argument
      g. Every law has a lawgiver.
      h. There is a moral law.
      i. Therefore, there is a moral lawgiver.

C. S. Lewis makes this case so clearly when he asserts, "Human beings, all over the earth, have this curious idea that they ought to behave in a certain way, and cannot really get rid of it. Secondly, that they do not in fact behave in that way. They know the Law of Nature; they break it. These two facts are the foundation."[34]

Every person in the world knows that courage, sharing, helping, saving, rescuing, protecting, loving, adopting, justice, honesty, and kindness are all more desirable and more preferred over cowardice, stealing, hurting, raping, kidnapping, abandoning, deceiving, lying, and rudeness. So, *how* do we all know this? How is it exactly that every human, regardless of where or when they live, knows what is good and what is evil? There's no purely evolutionary explanation for this.

Some will argue that we've evolved to know what is best for the survival of our species—that is, human beings. But Darwinian evolution only gets you to what's best for your group or tribe to survive. So, if what's best for your tribe is to smash in the skulls of your enemy's babies, then according to Darwinian evolution, there should be zero moral crime in this, zero shame, zero PTSD.

But why is it that we know Hitler was evil? According to Darwinian evolution, Hitler is just an example of survival of the fittest and natural selection, right? According to evolution, there are no grounds on which to condemn a person who uses their superior strength, intellect, and power to annihilate a weaker person. This is the major contradiction in Darwinian evolution. They will argue that the very same survival of the fittest and natural selection that has gotten us to where we are today is somehow morally evil now. According to whom? Is that just their opinion, or is there some transcendent moral law to which they are referring?

Of course, we know that there is. The law is written on the heart of every human (Rom 2:14–15) by the Law Giver himself. The very existence of such a transcendent law points to the existence of God.

4. DNA

If you're in an aircraft searching for someone on the ground and you see an SOS written in the sand, will you think that maybe the wind and water have created that message? Or what if you're walking through the woods and find a paperback book lying on the ground? Will you entertain the possibility that it has been formed by natural causes over millions of years?

Or what if you are exploring in a cave and see the images of stick men with spears painted on the walls of the cave? Will you conclude that those images have been created by forces of nature? Absolutely not! We all know that even the three-letter SOS scratched into the sand is a clear indication that an intelligent designer has authored that message. We all know that the pages and paragraphs of a book can only be the product of an intelligent mind. And we all know that pictures on a cave wall mean that someone has been in that cave before we have, and they made that by their own handiwork. As intuitively obvious as these three examples are, there are people who choose to believe that the longest, most complex message in the universe has just happened to write itself from nothing.

Each cell in your body contains a word that is 6.4 billion letters long of DNA. A, C, T, and G are the four letters that repeat in unique patterns in the DNA of every one of us—and no two are exactly alike. You would need about 2,064 Bibles to contain all the letters found in each cell of your body! It will take an entire library to contain that one word. And that word is the digitally coded message that's written in each one of your thirty trillion cells!

Bill Gates, the founder of Microsoft, said, "DNA is like a computer program but far, far more advanced than any software ever created."[35] So, if an SOS on the sand cannot possibly create itself out of nothing, then how much more does your DNA, something more advanced than any computer software ever created, require an intelligent designer?

The truth, of course, is that we are wonderfully made by a Supreme Being who has crafted us together while we were in our mother's womb (Ps 139:13–16). We are far more complex than any book or painting, and our very existence demands the existence of an author.

APPENDIX 2
EVIDENCE FOR
CHRISTIANITY

Christianity is the best explanation for historical facts. This is known as the *minimal facts argument* and is attributed to the work of Dr. Gary Habermas.[36] It uses only facts that even the atheist scholars and *nonbiblical historical sources agree on.* No other worldview offers a plausible explanation for these facts.

1. Jesus of Nazareth died by Roman crucifixion.
2. He was buried in a private tomb.

3. His tomb was found empty soon after his internment.

4. The disciples had experiences that *they believed* were actual appearances of the risen Jesus.

5. Because of these experiences, the disciples' lives were thoroughly transformed, even being willing to die for it.

Bonus fact 6: First-century skeptics James (the half-brother of Jesus) and Saul of Tarsus (also called Paul) were converted and became church planters, who were killed for their claims to have seen the risen Jesus.

Bonus fact 7: The Christian church has explosively grown into the most global, multicultural movement that the world has ever seen, despite the notoriously unpopular message of giving your money to the poor, sexual abstinence, and promised persecution (unlike other religions that have historically promised multiple wives and the spoils of war).

Christianity is the best explanation for these pieces of historical evidence.

Only Muslims deny fact 1. They have the swoon theory and the replacement theory, neither of which has any historical evidence, and both were developed about six hundred years after Jesus's death.[37]

So, the question for the skeptic is "Do you have a better explanation for these five historical facts?" If so, I'd love to hear it. What you will likely find is a piecemeal list of conspiracy theories that have no motives, witnesses, recorded accounts, or evidence. Therefore, Christianity is the best explanation of the evidence.

In addition to the minimal facts argument, there are also several pieces of evidence that support the veracity of the resurrection manuscripts. Here are five important pieces of evidence:

1. Embarrassing information. If a person makes up a lie, they don't make up things that make them look bad. However, the writers of the New Testament include numerous embarrassing stories about themselves, such as Jesus called Peter Satan (Mt 16:23), the disciples couldn't stay awake when Jesus asked them to pray (Mt 26:40), the disciples were not able to understand the meaning of Jesus's parables

(Mk 8:21), and the disciples panicked during the storm (Mt 8:25–26). Fabricated stories make the author sound flawless and special.

2. Women's testimony. In first-century Palestine, women's testimony was not even admissible in court. Women were not considered reliable witnesses. So, if you were making this story up, you would not have women as the ones to find the tomb empty and then running to tell the men. If men made up this story, they certainly would have cast themselves as the stars, not the women.

3. Terrible sales pitch. Christianity asks that you give your money to the poor and remain either celibate or monogamous and promises persecution and trouble to all who follow Jesus. On top of that, Jesus and all his disciples were tortured and killed, and we're supposed to be like them. If you were making up a religion, you would say the opposite of all this. You would promise wealth, women, and power (like Mormons and Muslims have historically done). Christianity is a terrible sales pitch, and this is further evidence that it is not man-made.

4. Multiple sources. Every other major religion is the result of *one* man (Joseph Smith, Muhammed, Buddha, Krishna, et al.) claiming that God has spoken to them and revealed a new message, religion, or path. The resurrection story of Jesus is collaborated by numerous authors: Matthew, Mark, Luke, John, Paul, Peter, James, and Jude. Many men from different backgrounds and upbringings all agree on the resurrection of Jesus. If you're going to fabricate a story, it's better to do it by yourself.

5. No motive. The disciples and authors of the New Testament had no motive, no reward, and nothing to benefit from proclaiming the resurrection and deity of Jesus. They were imprisoned, beaten, and killed. Any conspiracy theorist who thinks the resurrection story has been invented must be able to provide a motive for so many different people concocting and sticking to a story that will not get them any money, women, or power but only bring them persecution. The same cannot be said for Joseph Smith (who had thirty to forty wives)[38] or Muhammed (who had eleven wives, one of whom was nine years old)[39] after starting their own religions.

APPENDIX 3
THE TWELVE MEN'S
ALLIANCE MEMORY VERSES

LEAD YOUR FAMILY IN LEARNING ONE EACH MONTH

January: Romans 3:23, "For all have sinned and fallen short of the glory of God."

February: Romans 6:23, "For the wages of sin is death, but the gift of God is eternal life in Christ Jesus our Lord."

March: Romans 5:8, "But God demonstrates his own love for us in this: While we were still sinners, Christ died for us."

April: Romans 10:9, "If you confess with your mouth, 'Jesus is Lord,' and believe in your heart that God raised him from the dead, you will be saved."

May: Romans 10:13, "Everyone who calls on the name of the Lord will be saved."

June: John 3:16, "For God so loved the world that he gave his one and only Son, that whoever believes in him shall not perish but have eternal life."

July: Colossians 1:15, "The Son is the image of the invisible God, the firstborn over all creation."

August: Ephesians 2:8–9, "For it is by grace you have been saved, through faith—and this is not from yourselves, it is the gift of God—not by works, so that no one can boast."

September: John 14:6, "Jesus answered, 'I am the way and the truth and the life. No one comes to the Father except through me.'"

October: Acts 4:12, "Salvation is found in no one else, for there is no other name under heaven given to mankind by which we must be saved."

November: John 16:33, "I have told you these things, so that in me you may have peace. In this world you will have trouble. But take heart! I have overcome the world."

December: Hebrews 12:1–2, "Therefore, since we are surrounded by such a great cloud of witnesses, let us throw off everything that hinders and the sin that so easily entangles. And let us run with perseverance the race marked out for us, fixing our eyes on Jesus, the pioneer and perfecter of faith. For the joy set before him he endured the cross, scorning its shame, and sat down at the right hand of the throne of God."

APPENDIX 4
HOW TO SHARE THE GOSPEL USING ROMANS ROAD

1. "FOR ALL HAVE SINNED AND FALL SHORT OF THE GLORY OF GOD" (ROM 3:23).

Do you believe that people who commit moral crimes ought to be punished? Have you ever told a lie? Have you ever stolen anything (even time from your boss)? So, we're both liars and thieves. Jesus has said that even hating someone is a sin, and looking lustfully at a woman also is a sin. So, it goes beyond our actions. Even our thoughts disqualify us. We are all sinners, every one of us. We are all born as sinners into a broken, sinful world. We deserve punishment for our moral sins. That's what I call bad news!

2. "FOR THE WAGES OF SIN IS DEATH, BUT THE GIFT OF GOD IS ETERNAL LIFE IN CHRIST JESUS OUR LORD" (ROM 6:23).

The payment for our sins is death—eternal separation from God. But God has given us the gift of eternal life! But like all gifts, it must be accepted. It is not forced on us. And it is only available from one person, Jesus Christ!

3. "BUT GOD DEMONSTRATES HIS OWN LOVE FOR US IN THIS: WHILE WE WERE STILL SIN- NERS, CHRIST DIED FOR US" (ROM 5:8).

Why did Jesus Christ die? Because he was making the payment for our sins—yours and mine! And we did nothing to deserve it.

4. "IF YOU DECLARE WITH YOUR MOUTH, 'JESUS IS LORD,' AND BELIEVE IN YOUR HEART THAT GOD RAISED HIM FROM THE DEAD, YOU WILL BE SAVED" (ROM 10:9).

All that we have to do to receive this free gift of eter- nal life is believe that Jesus is Lord and that he has risen from the dead. It's a gift that has been paid in full already. It cannot be earned—just accepted. Now, that's what I call good news!

5. "EVERYONE WHO CALLS ON THE NAME OF THE LORD WILL BE SAVED" (ROM 10:13).

The gift is for everyone! And all we have to do is call on him! Is that something that you want to do right now?

> Dear God, I am a sinner in need of a savior. Please credit the death of your Son, Jesus Christ, to my account. I believe in your death and resurrection as payment for my sin, and I declare that you are my Lord.

I'll leave you with the most famous verse in the Bible. But I hope you'll hear it in a brand-new way today: "For God so loved the world that he gave his one and only son, that whoever believes in him shall not perish but have eternal life" (John 3:16).

APPENDIX 5
WHY ARE YOU A
CHRISTIAN?

This simple question can stump a lot of Christians. It's the *why* that causes a lot of folks to pause and actually consider why they believe what they do, not *how* they have come to be a Christian. That's their testimony. But *why* are we choosing to be a follower of Jesus today?

If we don't know our why, then we're susceptible to drifting off course when the storms of life hit. Doubt is a common part of the human experience. There's nothing wrong with confronting our doubt. In fact, it's healthy to examine our doubt and to answer it. Therefore, I want to offer you my why so that you can internalize it if you choose to make it yours as well. It's not based on feelings, as we have explained earlier, but rather on facts—on evidence. And it goes like this:

Q: Why are you a Christian?
A: Because it's true.

Q: How do you know that it's true?
A: Because of the evidence.

Q: What evidence?
A: Well, I'm glad you asked. The evidence is the multiple early recorded eyewitness testimonies (MERET, if that helps you remember).

The multiple firsthand eyewitness accounts of Matthew, John, Peter, Paul, and James all collaborate the same facts (see appendix 2), and the secondhand accounts of Mark and Luke support these claims as well from the eyewitnesses of Peter and Paul, respectively.

These accounts were recorded quite early compared with any other historical biographies. All the gospels were completed between estimates of AD 30–50 for Mark and AD 90 for John. So, within about ten years of Jesus's resurrection, we had early creeds (Corinthians, Philippians) circulating. And within sixty years of Jesus's resurrection, we had four biographies written and being translated into various languages. Compare this with the four hundred years it took to write the first biography of Alexander the Great, and you'll see that we have *multiple early recorded eyewitness testimonies* by men who had no motive to lie. It cost them their very lives, yet they never recanted, never got rich, never obtained power or women, and never wavered from their claim of seeing Jesus risen from the dead.

Now, that's pretty good evidence that a story is true. And it's evidence that no other religion has.

In closing, we should also hold people to the same standard that they hold us—that is, to ask them what evidence they have for their beliefs. You think the disciples stole Jesus's body? What evidence do you have? You think perhaps Jesus didn't really die or maybe had an identical twin? Interesting theory. What evidence do you have for that? Infinite number of universes? What's your evidence? Jesus never existed? What's your evidence?

You see, only Christianity enjoys the wealth of evidence found in having multiple early recorded eyewitness testimonies. Sure, people are free to believe whatever they want, but I require evidence for my beliefs, and that's why I'm a Christian. Christianity has evidence—not just theories and feelings.

NOTES

NOTES

NOTES

NOTES

ENDNOTES

1   J. Warner Wallace, "Are Young People Really Leaving Christianity?" *Cold-Case Christianity*, last modified October 30, 2021, https://coldcasechristianity.com/writings/are-young-people-really-leaving-christianity/.

2   Alister McGrath, *Mere Apologetics: How to Help Seekers and Skeptics Find Faith* (Grand Rapids, Michigan: Baker Publishing Group, 2012).

3   McGrath, *Mere Apologetics*.

4   C. S. Lewis, *Mere Christianity* (C. S. Lewis Pte Ltd, 1942, 1943, 1944, 1952). Extract used with permission.

5   J. P. Moreland, *Scientism and Secularism: Learning How to Respond to a Dangerous Ideology* (Wheaton, Illinois: Crossway, 2018).

6   Moreland, *Scientism and Secularism*.

7   Frank Turek, *Stealing from God: Why Atheists Need God to Make Their Case* (Colorado Springs, Colorado: NavPress, 2014).

8   Gregory Koukl, *The Story of Reality: How the World Began, How It Ends, and Everything Important That Happens in Between* (Grand Rapids, Michigan: Zondervan, 2017).

9   Austin Gentry, *Ten Things Every Christian Should Know for College: A Student's Guide on Doubt, Community, and Identity* (Middletown, Delaware: Gentry Publishing, 2018).

10 John C. Lennox, *Seven Days That Divide the World: The Beginning According to Genesis and Science* (Grand Rapids, Michigan: Zondervan, 2007).

11 Norman Geisler and Frank Turek, *I Don't Have Enough Faith to Be an Atheist* (Wheaton, Illinois: Crossway, 2004).

12 Gregory Koukl, *Tactics*, 10th anniversary ed. (Grand Rapids, Michigan: Zondervan, 2019).

13 Koukl, *Tactics*.

14 Andy Stanley, *Irresistible: Reclaiming the New That Jesus Unleashed for the World* (Grand Rapids, Michigan: Zondervan, 2018).

15 https://carm.org/bible-difficulties/if-jesus-is-god-why-did-he-not-know-the-hour-of-his-return-day/.

16 Norman Geisler and Thomas Howe, *The Big Book of Bible Difficulties: Clear Concise Answers from Genesis to Revelation* (Grand Rapids, Michigan: Baker Publishing Group, 1992).

17 Alan Axelrod and Charles Phillips, *Encyclopedia of Wars* (New York: Facts on File, 2005).

18 Koukl, *Tactics*.

19 William Federer, *What Every American Needs to Know about the Qu'ran: A History of Islam and the United States* (Amerisearch Inc., 2007).

20 J. Warner Wallace, *Cold-Case Christianity: A Homicide Detective Investigates the Claims of the Gospels* (Colorado Springs, Colorado: David C. Cook, 2013).

21 Wallace, *Cold-Case Christianity*.

22 Richard Dawkins, *The God Delusion* (London: Bantam Press, 2006).

23 William Lane Craig, YouTube video, https://www.youtube.com/watch?v=6CulBuMCLg0&t=11s.

24 John C. Lennox, *God's Undertaker: Has Science Buried God?* (Oxford, England: Lion Hudson, 2009).

25 Antony Flew, *There Is a God: How the World's Most Notorious Atheist Changed His Mind* (New York, New York: HarperCollins Publishers, 2007).

26 John C. Lennox, *Can Science Explain Everything?* (Denmark: Good Book Company, 2019).

27 Alvin Plantinga, *God, Freedom, and Evil* (Grand Rapids, Michigan: William B. Eerdmans Publishing Company, 1974).

28 Richard Dawkins, *River Out of Eden* (New York: Basic Books, 1995).

29 Charles Colson, *Born Again* (Grand Rapids, Michigan: Baker Publishing Group, 1976).

30 https://www.compellingtruth.org/teleological-argument-existence-God.html.

31 Ibid.

32 Isaac Newton, "General Scholium," in *Mathematical Principles of Natural Philosophy* in *Great Books of the Western World*, ed. Robert Hutchins (Chicago: Encyclopedia Britannica).

33 Geisler and Turek, *I Don't Have Enough Faith*.

34 Lewis, *Mere Christianity*.

35 Bill Gates, *The Road Ahead* (New York, New York: Viking Penguin Press, 1995).

36 Gary Habermas and Michael Licona, *The Case for the Resurrection of Jesus* (Grand Rapids, Michigan: Kregel Publications, 2004).

37 Nabeel Qureshi, *No God but One: Allah or Jesus?* (Grand Rapids, Michigan: Zondervan, 2016).

38 *Michael Quinn, The Mormon Hierarchy: Origins of Power (Salt Lake City, UT: Signature, 1994).*

39 Federer, *What Every American …*

ABOUT THE AUTHOR

David Mills is the founder and director of Men's Alliance, a national men's ministry where tribes of men across the country meet weekly for rugged, outdoor workouts and real-world devotions around a fire. He and his wife, Kerry, have been married since 2000, and have four children. He is a retired Air Force officer who is now a missionary to men in America.

Printed in the United States
by Baker & Taylor Publisher Services

Printed in the United States
by Baker & Taylor Publisher Services